Sammy's Walks

Dog walks in the Forest of Dean

2016

by Cheryl Mayo and Sammy

With many thanks to our fellow walkers, Rob and Jim, for their willingness to get lost in the woods.

© Cheryl R Mayo 2016.

Contains Ordnance Survey data
© Crown copyright and database right [2016]

Published by Holborn House Ltd January 2016.

Oakdean, High Street, Blakeney, GL15 4DY

Introduction

This book is for dog walkers new to the Forest of Dean. You may have just moved here, or just acquired a dog. Or perhaps you are visiting and don't fancy spending half your holiday getting lost.

This book aims to help you enjoy your walks while learning your way around the Forest. To give you some context about where you are walking, I have also included little bites of history in places. But if you want to know more about the long and fascinating story of the Forest of Dean, look out for Christine Martyn's highly readable book, *The Forest Revisited; a Modern History*.

The walks described here are tried and tested and mainly keep to forestry tracks and waymarked paths. In describing the walks I have tried to be consistent in terminology: a track is a hard surfaced Forestry Commission track; a trail is wide and generally well surfaced but not normally suitable for vehicles; and a path is either narrow or rough surfaced, suitable only for walkers. All stiles have dog openings and can be walked around if necessary.

Before you start out, please read through the points about walking in the Forest of Dean shown overleaf.

This is the third edition of this book. The book has proved popular with locals, day visitors and holiday-makers alike. We expanded the first edition and in this book there are some new walks also, including two longer walks for those feeling very energetic (or who also own border collies!) and a list of very short, easy walks as well.

Through our blog, sammyswalks.holbornhouse.com, we will try to keep you updated on any changes to routes (eg if logging has affected paths). You can also post comments there if you see something of interest to other dog walkers, or you can email us at sammyswalks@outlook.com.

Sammy and I hope our book gives you hours of walking pleasure and we look forward to seeing you in the woods from time to time, as we often do.

Cheryl *Cheryl*

Sammy

Walking in the Forest

- The Dean is a working forest. So expect to find heavy machinery sometimes working nearby. Logging can also affect some routes, so we have set up a blog, *sammyswalks.holbornhouse.com* to keep you posted.
- Fences, stiles, waymark posts and even bridges are sometimes replaced, repaired or taken out. So if you come to a point where it says there's a stile and there's now a gate, don't worry - as long as everything else looks right.
- There are limited facilities: Beechenhurst and the Cycle Centre both have cafes and toilets, and there are toilets at Mallards Pike and (in summer only) at Wenchford.
- Beechenhurst, Mallards Pike and Wenchford have pay and display parking. If you live in the Forest it is worth buying a Discovery Pass which gives you free parking at any of the local Forestry Commission sites where there is normally a charge (go to *http://www.forestry.gov.uk/forestry/INFD-7W5Kq6*).
- When walking on the cycle trail be aware of cyclists and keep your dog under control.
- You will occasionally come across boar: put your dog on the lead and find another path.
- There are dog litter bins at most of the starting points. However, if you are in the middle of the Forest it is quite okay to use a stick to flick the mess off the path into the undergrowth. It is definitely not okay to leave plastic bags of dog mess lying around.
- Finally, the Forest can get very muddy in wet weather even on the main tracks, so always wear suitable footwear.

Summary

Start point		Walk	Length Km	Total uphill walking (metres)	Est time	Page
Wenchford		1	2.2	58	35 min	10
		2	3.8	92	1 hr	12
		3	5	116	1 ¼ hrs	14
	with option	3a	6.8	134	1 ½ hrs	
Mallards Pike		4	4.8	65	1 hr	20
		5	5.4	138	1 ½ hrs	22
	with option	5a	8.2	180	2 hrs	
Linear Park		6	4.0	71	1 hr	27
Cannop Ponds		7	4.7	150	1 ¼ hrs	31
		8	5.9	127	1 ½ hrs	34
Speech House: Arboretum		9	3.3	46	45 mins	40
	with option	9a	4.9	80	1 hr	
Speech House: Woodlands		10	5.0	80	1 ¼ hrs	43
		11	4.9	106	1 ¼ hrs	46
Soudley Ponds		12	3.8	114	1 hr	52
	with option	12a	5.8	191	1 ½ hrs	
Yorkley		13	4.1	100	1 hr	55
	with option	13a	5.7	147	1 ½ hrs	
Beechenhurst		14	3.8	83	55 min	59
	with option	14a	7.2	138	1hr 40min	
LongWalks	Beechenhurst	15	12.6	274	3 ¼ hrs	64
	Mallards Pike	16	13.5	235	3 ¼ hrs	70
Short Walks						74

Walk start points

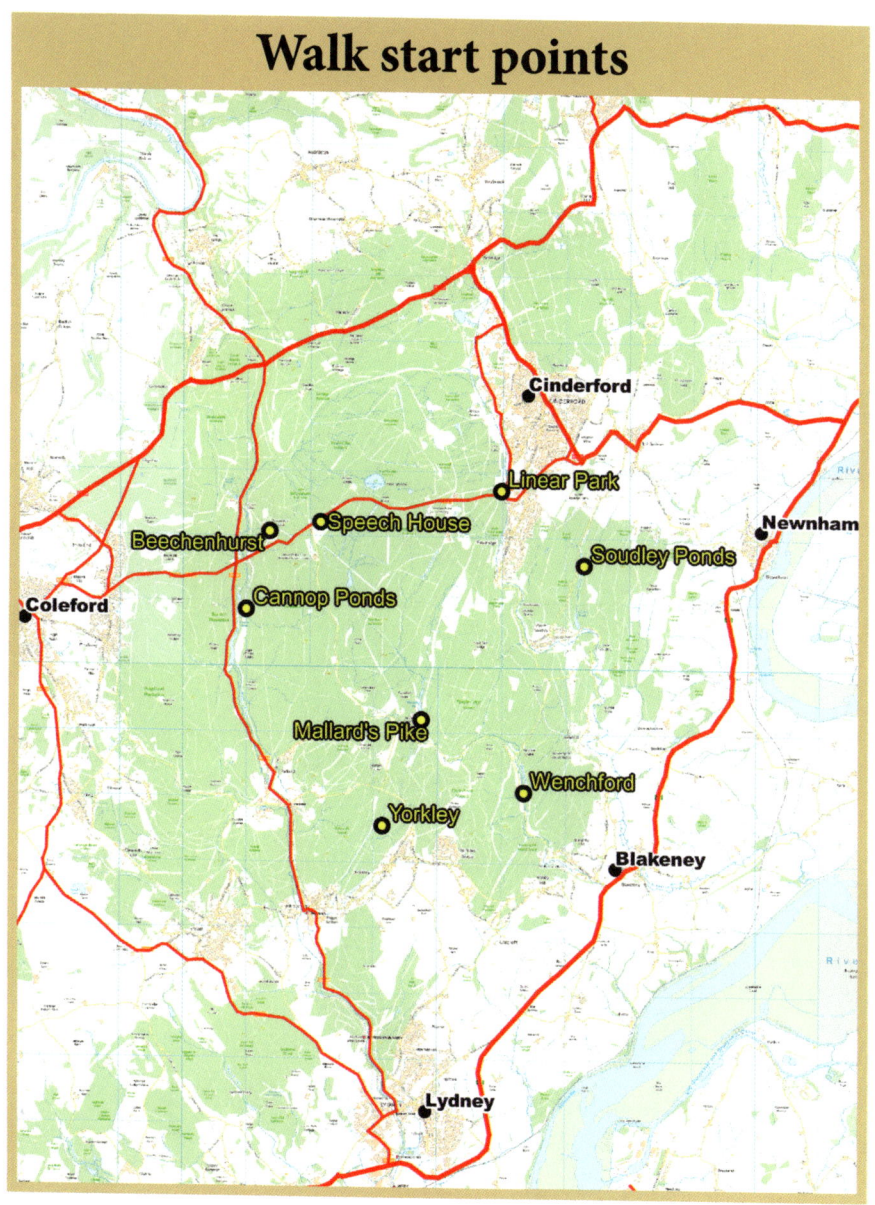

Wenchford

Walks from Wenchford

Wenchford is a popular local picnic site. The toilet block is open during the summer months and on some weekends there is also a burger van. Blackpool Brook runs through here and is shallow enough for small children to paddle happily. Pink balloons heralding birthday parties are quite common during the summer. However, for much of the year and during the week it is primarily the preserve of dog walkers.

Wenchford

In addition to the walks described here, you can

- » take the green waymarked Blackpool Brook trail, which loops along beside the brook and into the woods nearby, for just under 1 km;
- » stroll along the Brook, heading upstream along the picnic area, turning around at some point to retrace your steps;
- » take the link path to Mallards Pike, which is marked by white arrows. The return distance is 5 km, mostly along good forestry tracks. You do need to cross a road which has a blind corner, so remember the dog lead.

Location: From the A48 at Blakeney take the B4431 Parkend road. Two kilometres along this road you will find the site signposted on the right. The barrier is open and closed daily, with closing times varying depending on the time of year, so take note of the specific time as you drive in. OS Grid ref: SO 654081

There is pay and display parking during the summer months.

Wenchford

Walk 1 Start point: Wenchford carpark
Length 2.2 km, total uphill walking 58 metres, est time 35 mins

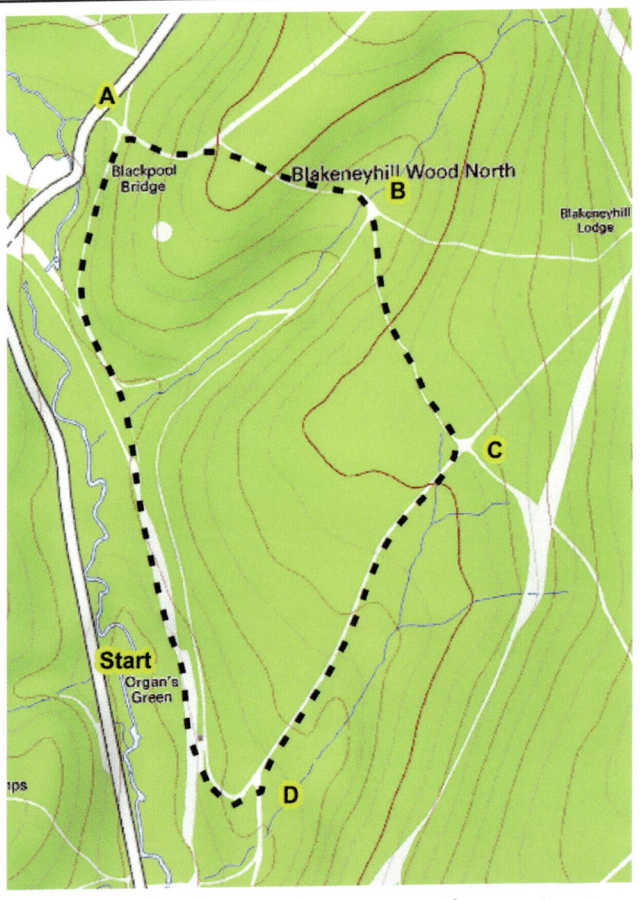

This undulating walk takes you along pretty paths, crossing streams and rivulets. It follows the Mallards Pike link for a while, and then returns via a forestry track.

With the toilet block on your right and the picnic area on your left, take the track straight ahead. At the end of the parking area, take the path ahead, past a large stone and go along it to reach a second parking area. A path down to Blackpool Brook goes off to your left, but ignore this and instead follow the sign to Mallards Pike, marked by a white arrow. The path goes down, crosses a small stream and then goes back up to a T-junction. Again fol-

10

Wenchford

low the Mallards Pike link sign, turning left and walking along a wide path with Blackpool Brook on your left.

Shortly after another link sign, the path forks (A). The link walk continues straight ahead, but instead of following this, take the right hand path up the slope to another fork. Again take the right hand path and, ignoring a narrow path off to your left, continue on this wider path. The path crests the hill and then goes fairly steeply down to the brook (B). Cross the brook and veer right to an intersection of paths. Go straight on and after a bit the path goes quite steeply uphill for a short distance before levelling out. Continue on to a forestry track (C). Turn right and follow the track gently downhill to a point where it bends to the left and descends sharply. Instead of continuing on down, look for a path to the right (D). Take the path and follow it as it bears right, back to the carpark and picnic area.

Wenchford

Walk 2 Start point: Wenchford carpark
Length 3.8 km, total uphill walking 92 metres, est time 1 hr

This walk starts with a gentle but steady climb before coming out to a forestry track which winds its way back down again in a wide loop.

With the toilet block on your left and your back to the picnic ground, look for the path up into the woods. Go up past a green waymark, and veer right to follow the path up and then around to the left to a forestry track (A). Walk up the track, going steadily uphill, to a junction of track and paths (B).

The main track continues around to the right, but ignore this and go straight ahead, continuing uphill. The path is crossed by a small rivulet which makes it boggy at times, but if you keep to the right you can avoid the worst of it. Continue on towards a large pylon which you can see ahead of you. The path ends at a grassy area, but go straight on with the pylon on your left, over another rather muddy patch, up a short slope and across a grassy area to a for-

Wenchford

estry track (C). Blakeney Hill Lodge is just to the left and directly ahead of you is a horse paddock which in spring is a mass of daffodils.

Turn right and walk along the track, passing a large enclosure on the left. The track eventually bends around to the right and goes downhill. Keep on the main track passing a number of paths on both sides. After a while the track curves again to the right. There is also a path going straight ahead, but keep to the main track, passing a fenced off disused quarry on your left, and continue steadily on down, passing under various sets of pylon and telegraph wires. The track then veers to the left and goes more steeply downhill, reaching the junction at point B.

Continue straight ahead onto a path, crossing a small stream. (*You can instead turn left and retrace your steps back to point A and the carpark at this point.*) About 100 metres in, look out on the left for a narrow path (there are two paths, separated by a mass of brambles, either will do). Take the path and follow it – it can be quite hard to see initially but just keep straight on and it becomes clearer – down through the trees. It becomes steeper towards the end, just before reaching a T-junction with another path. At this point you will see that you are just above the carpark and picnic area. Turn left and take any of the paths back down to your start point.

Wenchford

Walks 3 and 3a Start point: Wenchford carpark
3: *Length 5 km, total uphill walking 116 metres, est time 1¼ hours*
3a: *Join at Walk 2, point C, length 6.8km, est time 1 ½ hrs*

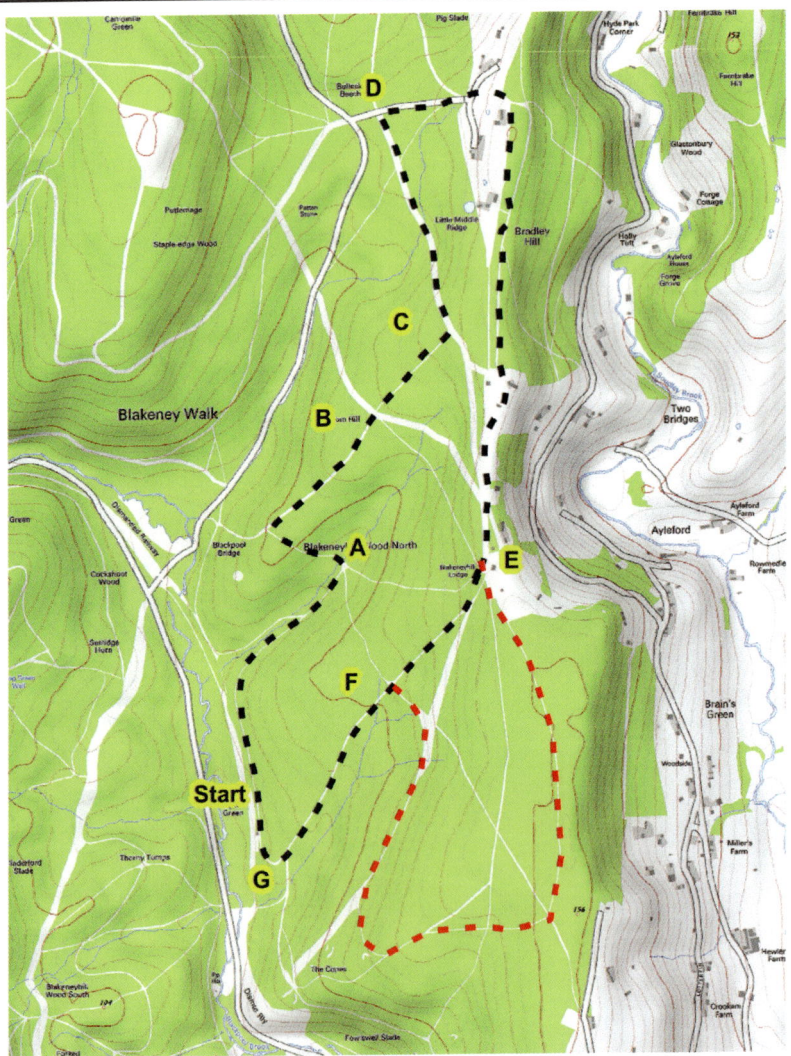

This walk involves some steady uphill work, but in the late spring you are rewarded with a walk through some of the most beautiful bluebell woods in the Forest. You also walk along a ridge line where you catch glimpses between the trees of wide views across the Severn. The longer option of the walk is a gentle downhill stroll on a good forestry track.

Wenchford

With the toilet block on your right and the picnic area on your left, take the track to the end of the carpark. Ignore the path straight ahead and look for a narrow uphill path on your right, going up here to a T-junction. Turn left and, ignoring the path which goes up to the right, continue on this path with the picnic area and Blackpool Brook below you on the left. Pass a path which goes left down to another parking area. Continue on, bending around to the right and with the brook below you on your left. Another path joins from the left. Keep straight on, on what is now a quite stony path, cross a rivulet (dry only in the driest weather) and shortly after this you come to a junction of paths (A).

Turn left down the hill and cross the brook. The path climbs steeply for about 100 metres and then levels out briefly before descending. You soon come to a point where a narrow path goes off to your right with a wider path just beyond it. Take the wider path, turning right, and follow it gently uphill. In late spring these woods are carpeted with bluebells and are quite popular with visitors and locals alike. The path takes you to a dirt road, with a 15 mph sign just to the left (B).

Cross the road (take care: vehicles are rare but tend to move quite

Bluebells above Wenchford

Wenchford

quickly) and continue uphill along the wide path directly ahead. The bluebells continue here as well. The path climbs steadily up and ends at a T-junction with a track (C).

Turn left and follow the track. *(You can shorten the walk here by turning right and continuing on the track to Blakeney Hill Lodge, point E. From here, you can either continue the main walk or take the option as described below.)* Continue on to eventually reach a metalled road (D). Turn right up the hill, past a white house on your right with a red letter box, enjoying the mass of daffodils on the verge throughout the spring. Just past the house you will see a wooden sign for Twilbee.

Keep the sign to your left and walk along the track (the metalled road ends here). You soon come to stables and the house Twilbee, set in charming grounds. Continue on and just at the point where the garden meets the horse paddock you come to a telegraph pole. A few metres past the telegraph pole there is a path off to the left. Take this to join another path. There has been some logging here and the path may still be a bit rough in places. Turn right and

keep on until the path ends at a track with houses ahead of you. Turn left, going past Bradley Hill Farmhouse, and continue down. Along this stretch you can catch glimpses between the trees of the countryside across to and beyond the River Severn. Go past a driveway and a gate with a sign Woodside House on your right and keep on, now joining a line of telegraph poles. Go past Hepworth Cottage to a junction, where a dirt road comes in from your right. Follow the line of the telegraph poles along the main track and shortly come to Blakeney Hill Lodge (E).

Option 3a: for a longer walk which takes you gently downhill on a forestry track, continue on past Blakeney Hill Lodge, joining at Walk 2, point C and following the instructions back to Wenchford.

Main walk continued

To continue this walk, leave the track just before you reach the Lodge and take the path which goes off at an angle on your right, next to the telegraph poles. It goes through large boulders and on to a pylon. Just as you reach the pylon, there is a path to the right. Take this and walk down (it is quite boggy in places) to arrive at a forestry track which comes in from the left and then bends to go on directly ahead of you (F). Take the track straight ahead, continuing downhill to a point where the track bends to the left and descends sharply. Instead of continuing on down, look for a path to the right (G). Take the path and follow it as it bears right, back to the carpark and picnic area.

Walks from Mallards Pike

Mallards Pike is a popular Forest beauty spot. The lake was built by the Forestry Commission as a tourist attraction and is named after a Mr Maller, a toll-keeper who lived in a cottage near what is now the entrance to the site. Today visitors can simply sit by the lake and enjoy watching the ducks, or take to the high ropes on the Go-Ape course. Or use it as a very popular dog walk starting point. There are toilets open all year round and a burger van during summer weekends and holidays. Parking is pay and display. In addition to the walks described here you can

Mallards Pike

- » stroll around the lake edge;
- » follow the 6 km circular Adidas Running Trail;
- » take the link path to Wenchford, marked by white arrows. The return distance is 5 km.

There is also a 13 km walk from Mallards Pike in the long walks section of this book.

Location: From the A48 at Blakeney take the B4431 Parkend road. Five kilometres along this road you will find the site signposted on the right. The barrier is open and closed daily, with closing times varying depending on the time of year, so take note of the specific time as you drive in. OS Grid ref: SO 637093

Mallards Pike

Walk 4 Start point: Mallards Pike carpark
Length 4.8 km, total uphill walking 65 metres, est time 1hr

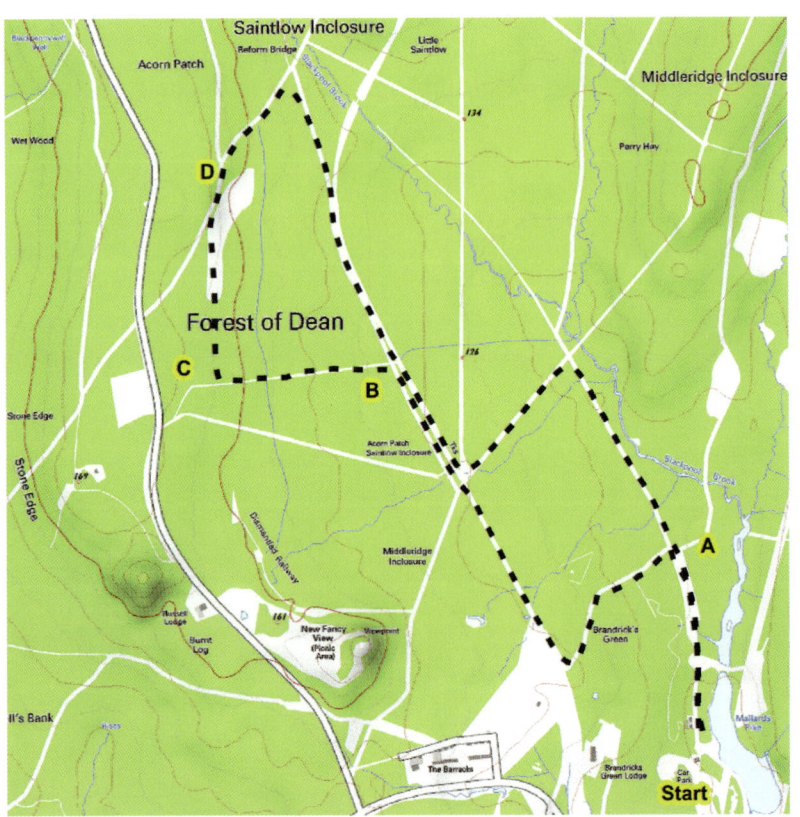

This is what I describe as a "flat walk" insofar as anywhere in the Forest can be described as flat. It is gentle, with varied scenery and using good trails or paths.

Keeping the Go Ape office on your left, walk to the beginning of the Running Trail and continue until the track divides into three (A). Take the first left (marked as the cycle trail) and follow the trail as it bends around to the right and then straight on to a signposted intersection. Turn left and then immediately right, so that you are now on the path parallel with the cycle trail.

Continue along the path, ignoring a grassy track which goes off at an angle on your left, until you come to a path on your left which slopes

Mallards Pike

gently upwards (B). Walk up the hill and, shortly after passing an enclosure on the left, look out for a grassy path off to the right (C). Take this path through pine trees until you come out onto a forestry track. Keep right to arrive at a fork in the track, with a sign to the left saying Trafalgar Avenue (D). Take the right hand track, down a short and steep hill. At the bottom take the track to your right. It soon begins to parallel the cycle trail. Keep on until you are back at the signposted intersection. Turn left, cross over the cycle trail, and at the next junction turn right. You are now back on the running trail, from where you can follow the signs to take you back to Mallards Pike Lake.

Mallards Pike

Walks 5 and 5a Start point: Mallards Pike carpark
5: Length 5.4 km, total uphill walking 138 metres, est time 1½ hrs
5a: Length 8.2 km, total uphill walking 180 metres, est time 2 hrs

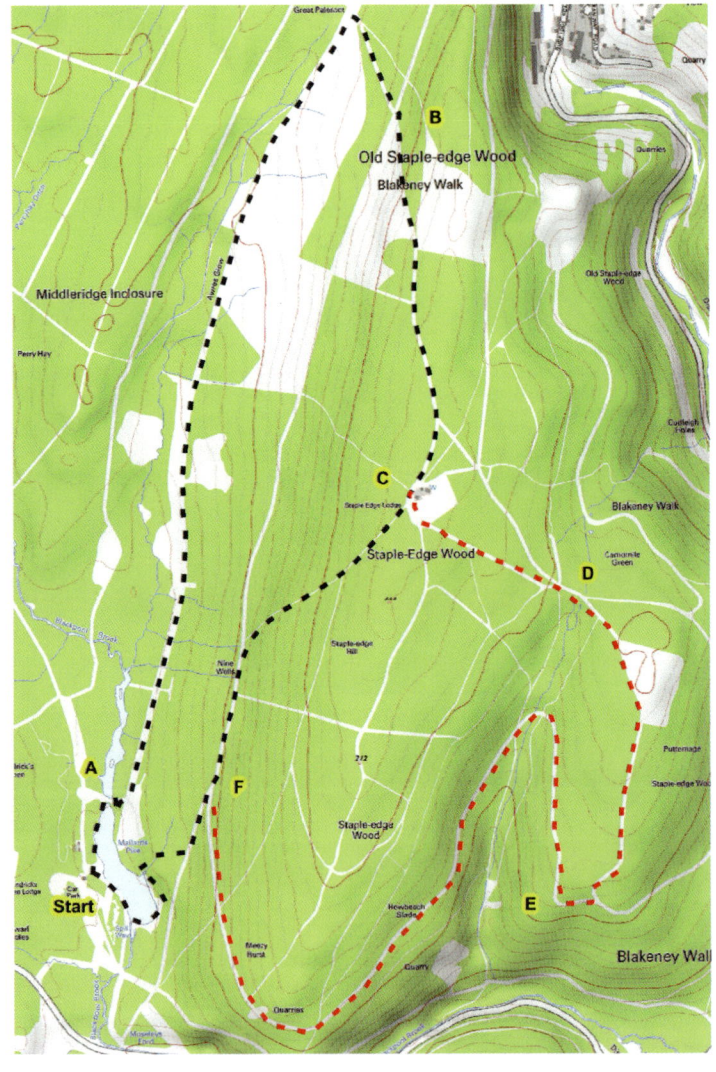

This walk takes you up to the ridge above Mallards Pike, the longish and steady climb being rewarded with far reaching views over the Forest. A steep grassy track brings you down from the ridge and from there it is a short distance back to the start point. The longer option follows good tracks as it winds its way gently downhill back to Mallards Pike.

Mallards Pike

Enjoying the dog dip

Walk down to the lake edge and follow the path to your left up to the boat ramp. Turn right to cross over the lake and then turn left, following the line of telegraph poles (A).

Continue along the track for about 2 kms to a T-junction. Turn right and go up the hill to a metal gate and stile (B). *Note: you can instead turn left at the T-junction and then left again to join the Running Trail, from where it is 3 kms back to Mallards Pike.* Cross the stile and then carry on straight over the intersection, continuing uphill, with a post and wire fence on your right.

The track levels out at a point where a considerable amount of clear felling has taken place on either side. The upside has been to reveal some far flung views across the Forest, especially beautiful in the autumn. Just past this clear felled area you come to Staple Edge Bungalows on your left, built in 1809 and still without electricity or mains water (C).

Decision point

To stay on the main walk, pass a waymark post on your right more or less opposite the Bungalows. A few metres past this, also on

Mallards Pike

your right, is a grassy path disappearing downhill.. Follow the path down to a fork, with a waymark post pointing back the way you have just come. Take the right hand path to go quite steeply down to a foresty track, with another waymark post. Turn left and follow the track gently downhill until you come to a wide fork, which is point F on this route. Take the right hand track downhill and follow the main walk instructions from point F below.

Option 5a

For the longer option, pass Staple Edge Bungalows and keep to the main track, going gently downhill. The track meets an intersection where there has been some recent clearing on the opposite side. Bear right, continuing downhill and past a gate perched by itself on the right of the track (D). To the left is a small, fenced pond with a rough path going past it. Ignore the path and stay on the main track. At a point where the track goes steeply downhill and bends to the left, turn sharp right (E) and continue on this new track, which winds its way around the hill.

Towards the end of this section, take in the wide views to your left. Just past a large grove of conifers on your left there is a path which intersects the main track. Cross over this and shortly afterwards the track bends to the right, with another track coming in from the left (F). Turn left onto this track and then continue with the main walk instructions below.

Main walk continued

From point F, continue on down and just as the track levels out look for a waymark post with a white arrow pointing straight ahead, at the top of a path descending on your right. Take the path which goes down very steeply (and sometimes a bit slippery) to the lake, coming out right at the dog dip.

Turn left and follow the path back to the carpark.

Linear Park

A Walk from Linear Park

Linear Park is a conservation area at the edge of the Forest town of Cinderford and as such is very popular with local dog walkers. The lakes you will pass were created in 1990 and quickly attracted a variety of wildlife. There are no facilities.

Location: The entrance to Linear Park is located on a bend on the left, just off the B4226 (Speech House Road) immediately before entering Cinderford from the direction of the Speech House. The entrance is marked by an old railway bulk container at the former Ruspidge Halt station. OS Grid reference SO6412.

Linear Park

> **Walk 6 Start point: Linear Park, Cinderford**
> *Length 4 kms, total uphill walking 71 metres, est time 1 hr*

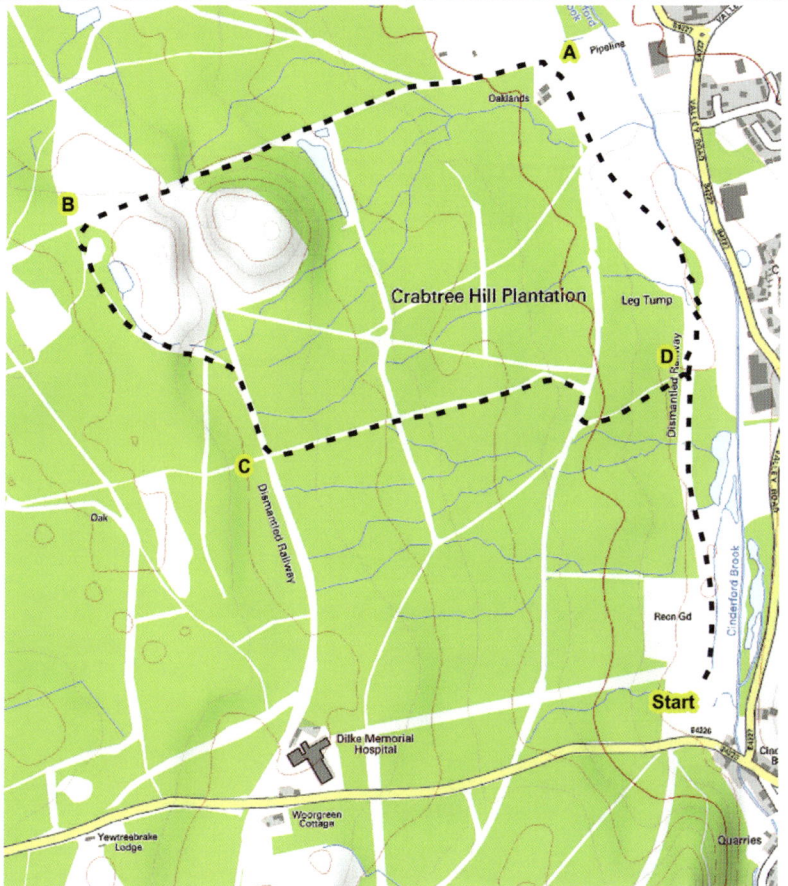

The start of this walk follows the line of the old railway and at one point takes you to a map and information board so you can see just what a busy industrial place it once was. You will also pass the remains of a once flourishing colliery.

From the carparking area nearest to the barrier, take the main path straight ahead, through the barrier. At the intersection, continue straight on, with views of Cinderford off to your right between mature oaks. Go past a cycle trail sign opposite

Linear Park

a rather bent-looking railway signal post on top of the old railway embankment, and keep on until you reach Bilson Halt. There is an information board here and photos of what it used to look like when the trail you are on was a working railway and much of the area was covered with working coal mines.

Not long past Bilson Halt you come to a rough road (A). Turn left (there might be the occasional car), going past a site with an old stone building and old trucks and vans. The road goes uphill and

bends to the left, then straight on, past a treatment works, to a forestry barrier. Go through the barrier onto a wide forestry track and keep on this, going gently uphill, passing a large pond on the left. Go straight on at the intersection where a rutted track goes steeply uphill on your left and continue uphill to the next intersection. The cycle trail crosses the track here (B). Turn left onto the cycle trail and immediately come to the remains of Foxes Bridge Colliery. If you're feeling fit, take the narrow steep path to the left, past the fenced-in shaft, and climb the short distance to the top of the old spoil heap. From here you have a lovely view of Cinderford, at least until the young pines grow up to block it out. Return to the cycle trail and continue along, shortly going downhill with the path gradually bearing to the left.

Keep on the trail as it does a sharp right bend and shortly afterwards come to a signpost with the number 9 on it, opposite a path to your left (C). Take the path (indicated Cinderford Linear Park 0.9 km) and go downhill to a T-junction. Turn right and then almost immediately left, following the cycle trail markers, and go downhill again to meet up with the path you started on (D). Either turn right and go straight back to the carpark, or cross over and then turn right to take the more rugged path which will also bring you back to the carpark.

Walks from Cannop Ponds

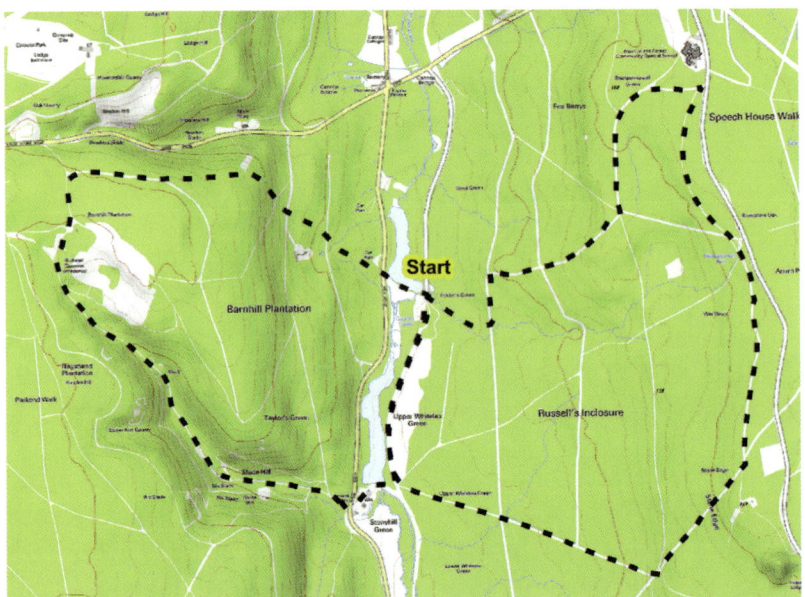

Cannop Ponds is a series of manmade lakes set in the steep sided Cannop Valley. It is a haven for birdlife and has a good population of swans and mandarin ducks. There is a picnic area and carparking, but no facilities except for a burger van on occasional summer weekends and holidays. Beechenhurst Lodge, with its cafe and toilets, is only a few minutes drive away however, as is the Cycle Centre.

In addition to the walks described here, you can take the path around the ponds. This can be narrow and rough in many places and one side runs close to the road so be aware of this if your dog has a tendency to run off.

Location: Enter from Speech House Road (B4226), and drive along the metalled road to reach the carpark and picnic area. OS Grid ref: SO610108

Cannop Ponds

Walk 7 Start point: Cannop Ponds carpark
Length 4.7 km , total uphill walking 150 metres, est time 1¼ hrs

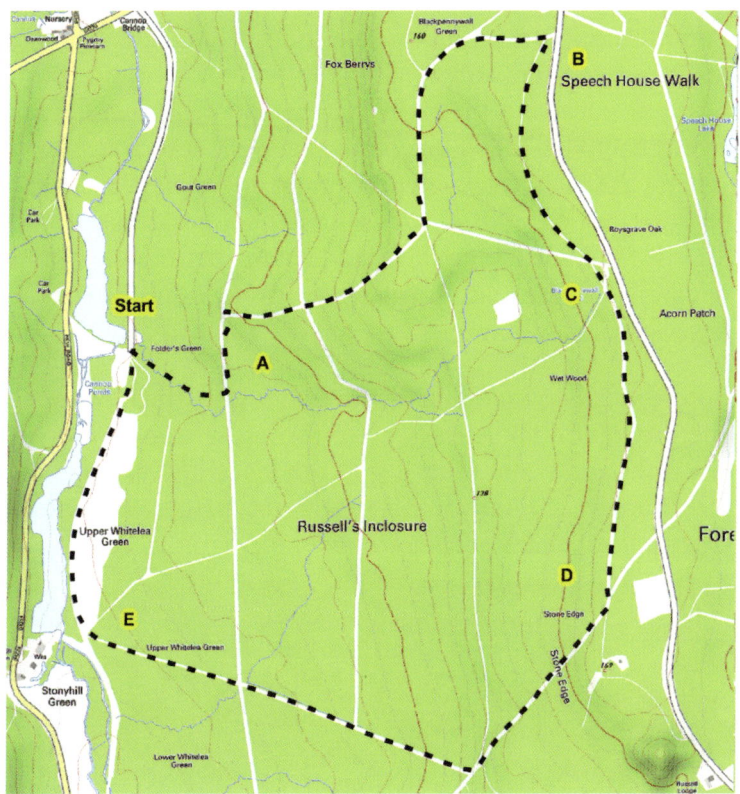

This walk starts out with a short sharp ascent on a rather rough path, then steadily climbs on a forestry track. You then have a level walk along the top of the valley before joining the cycle trail to descend back to the start point. On the way you will see the HMS Victory memorial.

As you enter the carpark one way system, there is a narrow path which goes off to the left about 30 metres or so in. Take this path and follow it across two bridges and then up and down above the stream until you reach a gate which leads onto a forestry track (A).

Turn left and gently ascend to a point where there is a track off to the right, waymarked with a yellow arrow, Gloucestershire Way and Beechenhurst Trail. Follow the direction of the yellow way-

Cannop Ponds

mark up the hill and continue to climb steadily to an intersection of tracks. Follow the yellow waymark direction straight ahead, still climbing. The track rises steeply for a short distance then starts to level out. Shortly after this the track forks. Take the left hand track, again following the yellow waymark direction. At this point there are mature conifers on your left and younger trees on your right. The track curves to the right and on the bend there is another waymarked post. This time, ignore the yellow waymark and continue on the main track. It curves right and then goes up to a gate and stile leading onto a road, with school buildings to your left (B). Just before reaching the road take the path to the right. Keep on, parallelling the road and going gently downhill. There are great views across the Cannop Valley to your right.

You eventually come to a T-junction with a track, with a gate a little way up on your left (C). Go through the gate, immediately turn right and come back inside the fence line through another gate directly ahead of you. Keep straight on, parallelling the road. At a couple of places you pass some rather large tree stumps which

Spillway at Cannop Wharf

can make ideal seats if you want to rest a while. Towards the end of this section you come across the HMS Victory memorial, to the left of the path, commemorating a special oak which stood here for 202 years.

Soon after the memorial, the path meets a track at a T-junction (D). Turn right and right again at the fork, following the main track downhill and passing a plantation of saplings on your left. Pass a sign warning cyclists of a right turn ahead and at the T-junction turn right to join the cycle trail. Continue downhill, past the Three Brothers sign. Follow the trail around to the right and then keep going all the way down, through a gate at one point and shortly after that arriving at a T-junction with a signpost at Cannop Wharf (E). Turn right and follow the cycle trail (direction Cycle Centre) back to the picnic area and carpark.

If you want to take the path along the edge of the Ponds, you can access this via a path to the left of the Cannop Wharf sign. There are various exit points back up to the cycle trail along the way.

Cannop Ponds

Walk 8 Start point: Cannop Ponds carpark
Length 5.9 km, total uphill walking 127 metres, est time 1½ hrs

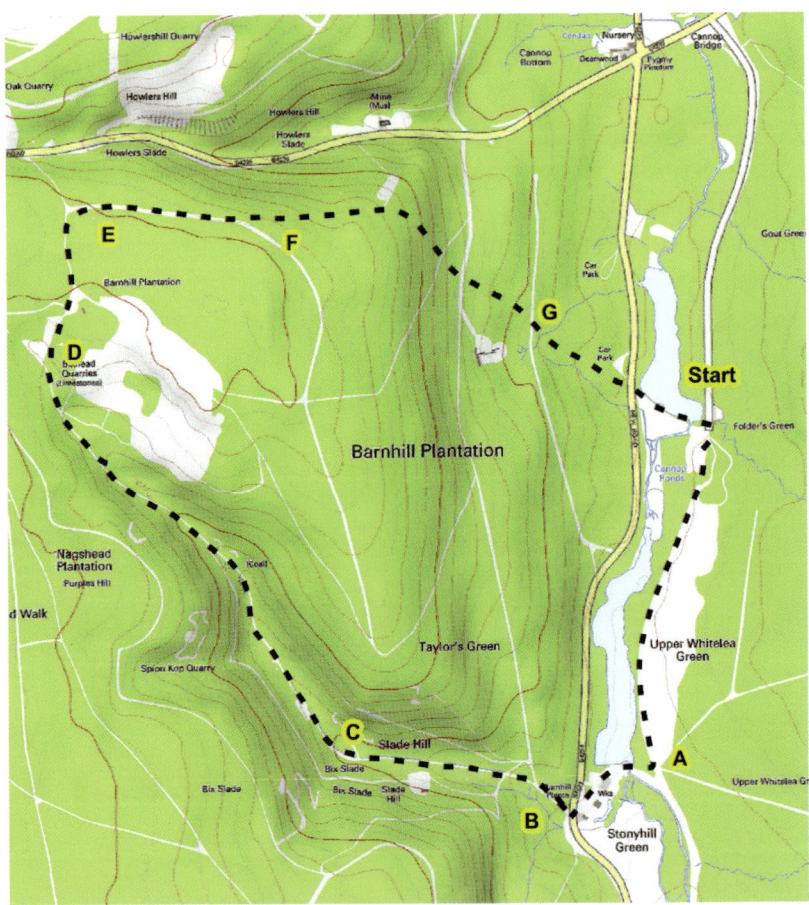

This walk starts out gently enough along the family cycle trail but then crosses the road into the Bixslade Valley to follow the old tramways route up the valley. The climb is well worth it as along the way you catch many glimpses of the Forest's mining heritage, passing quarries – many now defunct, some still in use – and old mine shafts, including a freeminer's gale which is still in operation. You then descend on a pretty waymarked path through the forest back down to Cannop Ponds.

Facing the ponds, walk left through the picnic area to the Family Cycle Trail (not marked, but you go past a wooden gate). Continue on until you reach a signposted junction and a sign for Cannop Wharf (A). Just after the sign take the path to your right which goes past the stone works and on up to the road. Cross the road (be careful, as this is a busy road and visibility either way is not good) and go through a barrier onto a forestry track. Now look out on the left for a path which goes beside a line of telegraph poles (B). Take this path, and you are now on the old tramways route up the valley. You can see many of the stone slabs which are still intact. Cross over a forestry track and continue on the old tram route until you come out onto a track which ends at the gates to a quarry on your right (C).

It is worth making a short detour here, turning left along the track to visit the monument to the United

Miners Memorial, Bixslade Valley

Cannop Ponds

Colliery Disaster of 1902. This is also the site of the still operating freeminer's coal mine (private property).

Return to the quarry gates and take the path to their left, through the large stones, following the telegraph poles. Continue steadily uphill, still on the old tramways route and still following the line of telegraph poles, passing a group of fenced disused mine shafts on your left and shortly afterwards a disused and overgrown quarry to your right. At the point where the telegraph poles follow a path to the left, ignore this and continue straight on. Not long after, the path levels out and enters an open area with a wire and stone fence directly ahead of you and a large quarry to the right. Take the path to the right of the fence, then the right fork so that you keep the quarry fence immediately on your right. You soon join a wide forestry track coming in from the left (D). There are quarry offices off to your right.

Go straight ahead, under the telegraph wires, and then turn left at the T-junction, along another wide track. Follow this to where it bends to the left and here go through the barrier to take the less well used track to the right (E). Here is a reward for your climb: the road appears a long way below you and across the forest you

Looking towards Cinderford with a glimpse of the Speech House

can see Cinderford in the distance and, closer in, a glimpse of the Speech House in amongst the trees.

Follow the track to a waymarked path off to the left (F), which marks the edge of the recently logged area, following this down into the trees and coming to the top of a fenced quarry. Follow the yellow arrow steeply down, with the fence on your left. At the point where the fence ends, the path bends to the right. Continue on quite steeply downhill, crossing a path and going straight on to reach a forestry track (G). Cross the track to take the yellow waymarked path, continuing downhill to a rather boggy patch. Here the path seems to lose itself, but if you keep going downhill, veering slightly right, you will pick it up again. Continue on to a waymarked post pointing straight ahead. Follow this, still going downhill, crossing a rivulet and keeping on the grassy path until you reach a layby opposite Cannop Ponds. Carefully cross the road, walk along the dam and back to the carpark.

Speech House

Walks from the Speech House

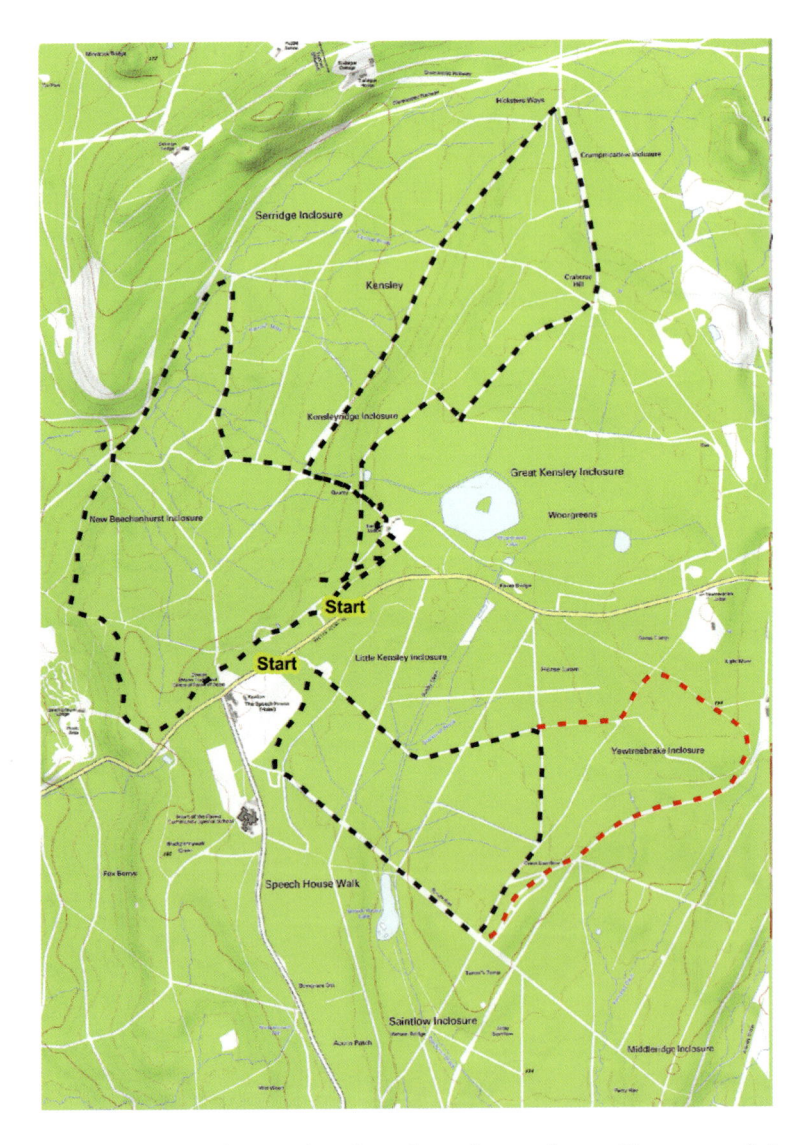

These walks are designed to be relatively gentle strolls, none of them being more than 5 km in length and involving little strenuous uphill walking. If you wish to push yourself and the dog harder, but in this same part of the Forest, then have a look at the walks from Beechenhurst and the two long walks at the end of the book. The first walk starts at the Cyril Hart Arboretum, located next to the Speech House. The Arboretum is named after a local historian and forestry expert and contains some 400 trees. Cyril Hart was also a Verderer of The Forest of Dean and the Speech House has been the traditional home of the Verderers' Court for over 300 years. Although now a hotel, the Court still meets there regularly. The Speech House is dog-friendly and a post walk visit to the Orangery for tea and cakes or a light lunch is well worthwhile.

The next two walks start at the the Speech House Woodlands carpark, just across the road from the Arboretum. There is a signed path from this carpark to Beechenhurst Lodge, a short distance away. Beechenhurst Lodge has toilets and a cafe, open all year round.

Location: The Arboretum carpark is on the B4226, just 200 metres along from the Speech House heading towards Cinderford. OS Grid ref: SO624118. The Speech House Woodlands carpark is a few metres further on, on your left. OS Grid ref: SO624125.

Spruce Ride in winter

Speech House

Walks 9 and 9a Start point: Cyril Hart Arboretum carpark
9: Length 3.3 km, total uphill walking 46 metres, est time 45 mins
9a: Length 4.9 km, total uphill walking 80 metres, est time 1 hr

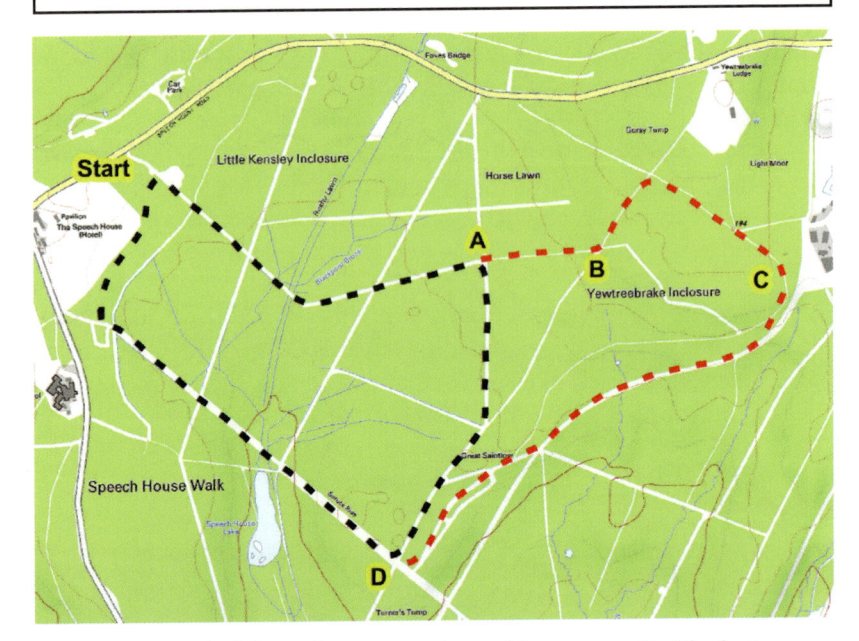

This walk mostly follows forestry tracks and is very gentle. The last section is along Spruce Ride, an avenue of mature cherry trees which provide a spectacular pink display in the spring. You also take in Speech House Lake, surrounded by mature trees which provide their own spectacular display in the autumn.

From the carpark, go through the gate into the Arboretum and head straight across to the opposite gate. Go down the path and straight across the next intersection. There is a cleared area of forest to your left. The path curves left and then straightens out. At the next intersection cross straight over. The next intersection has a large oak in the middle of it (A).

Decision point

To continue the main walk, turn right and follow the track down to a junction where another track comes in from the left. Continue on, passing a path coming in from the left and then reaching an intersection with a wide track, at the brow of a hill (D). This is Spruce Ride. Turn right and follow the instructions for the main walk from point D back to the carpark.

Option 9a

To take the option, go straight over at the intersection with the oak. Soon afterwards you come to a wide area with two paths coming in from the left and the path you are on curving around to the right (B). Take the first path left which goes gently uphill to an intersection with an enclosure on your left. Turn right and follow the path, with young trees on your right and towering conifers on your left. Pass between two large stones and at the fork go right, downhill. As the path levels out the cycle trail comes in from your left (C), marked by a cycle trail post. Just to the right is a short 'Bikes 'n' Berms' trail.

Continue on the cycle trail, going steadily downhill, passing a path on your right with a double wooden fence and then another one on your left as the trail bends to the right. After a while the trail is fenced on either side. Continue on to an intersection with a

Spruce Ride in spring

Speech House

Speech House Lake

track, and warning posts for cyclists. Here leave the cycle trail and turn right and then shortly afterwards come to a fork. Take the left hand path, going through an area where the track is divided by a small island of conifers bordered with logs.

The divided track comes together again just as you reach a T-junction with a forestry track. This is Spruce Ride. Turn right, and rejoin the main walk at the nearby intersection (D).

Main walk continued

From D, continue all the way down the long straight avenue to a gate at the end. About halfway, at the bottom of the dip, you pass Speech House Lake on the left.

Go through the gate into a parking area and then look to your right for the gate into the Arboretum. Go through and take any path, meandering through the trees with Speech House Field on your left, and back to the carpark.

Speech House

Walk 10 Start point: Speech House Woodlands car park carpark
10: Length 5 km, Total uphill walking 80 metres, Estimated time 1¼ hrs

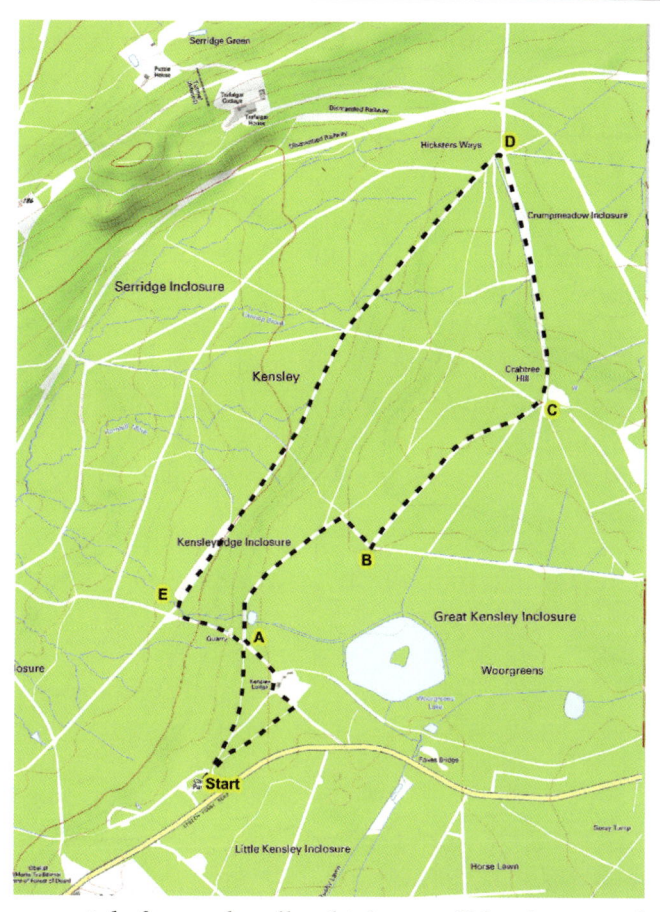

This is a straightforward walk which can all be done on forestry tracks, so good to do if the weather has been very wet. It includes three of the sculptures in the Sculpture Trail, but if you wish to see more of those, follow Walk 11, or do the whole of the trail (see walks from Beechenhurst).

With Speech House Road on your right, walk along the path to the yellow waymarked post and then take the right hand path, keeping the blue marker on your left, to go towards the stained glass 'Cathedral' sculpture. Just before the sculpture, turn left and fol-

Speech House

low the blue markers to the track by Kensley Lodge. Turn left on the track, passing a gate on your right, to go downhill and through a gate (A). Take the right hand track and follow this past a pond and a yellow waymark on the right. Keep on, passing another waymark on your left, until the track bends around to the right. There is a Gloucestershire Way marker indicating a path directly ahead, but ignore this and keep on the main track which soon starts to bend to the left (B).

On the bend there is a path going off to the left. Follow this across the open heathland, watching out for deer which can frequently be seen here, and coming out at a tarmac road (C) where you turn left. *Note: If the weather has been very wet and you wish to stay on hard tracks, then simply stay on the main track which goes straight for a time then curves to the left, with a smaller track going straight on. Keep to the main track which shortly becomes a tarmac road. As you crest the hill you will see tracks going off to the right and left. This is point C.*

Follow the tarmac road down quite steeply to a forestry track which goes off to the left, just before two large stones at the side of the road (D).

Take the left track, and about 100 metres in you will come to a fork, with a Gloucestershire Way marker and arrow on the left. Take the left fork, ie straight ahead, and continue for some time on this relatively flat track. Initially it takes you through mixed woodland, mostly beech with a scattering of larch and oak, so particularly lovely in autumn. You then go past an enclosure on your left. After the enclosure, there are more mature trees, and then you come to an intersection (E) with a post saying C2 on the opposite bank.

Turn left, up the steep hill, in the direction of the blue arrow. *Note: If you want to see the 'Hill 33' sculpture, take a short detour to the right, down the hill, but then return to point E.*

Towards the top of the hill you will pass the 'Echo' sculpture on your left, worth a detour to inspect closely. Continue up to the gate at A.

Just before this gate there is a path off to the right, marked the Gloucestershire Way. Take this path back to the carpark, but if it looks very muddy, the drier alternative is to simply keep straight on, retracing your steps and following the blue markers or the yellow waymarks back to the carpark.

Speech House

Walk 11 Start point Speech House Woodlands carpark
Length 4.9 kms Uphill walking 106 metres Est time 1¼ hrs

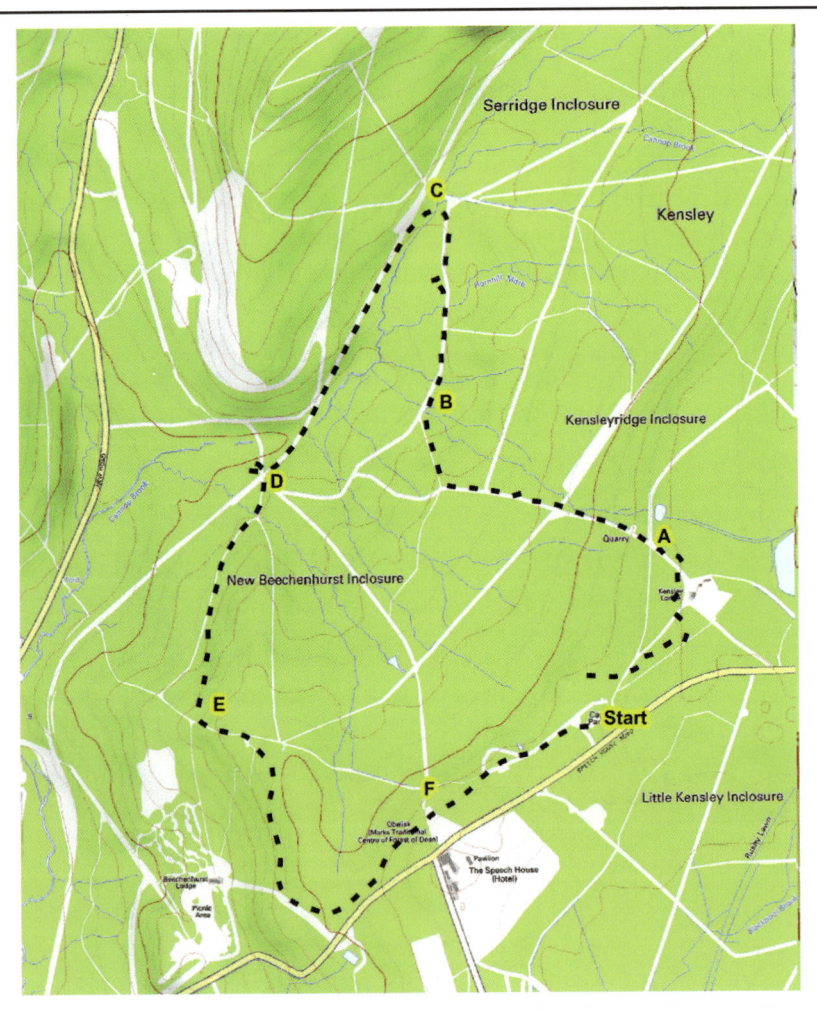

I designed this leisurely ramble after taking my daughter and some of her friends - down from London for some dog walking and autumn colour - on a walk with the aim of taking in as many of the Sculpture Trail works as we could manage in an hour or so. It's a very pleasant walk, not far, but with many stops, and mainly on forestry tracks. It also provides the option of stopping at the dog friendly Speech House for coffee or lunch. Visit www.forestofdean-sculpture.org.uk/sculptures for full descriptions of the various sculptures mentioned.

Speech House

With Speech House Road on your right, walk along the path to the yellow waymarked post and then take the right hand path, going towards the stained glass 'Cathedral' sculpture, which depicts many scenes of Forest life (it was done before the wild boar arrived, so you will search in vain for those). Just before the sculpture take the left path and follow the blue markers to the track by the house, Kensley Lodge (one of the old Forestry Commission lodges). Turn left, passing a gate on your right, to go downhill to the gates (A).

Go through and then keep straight on, downhill, soon coming to the clever and beautiful 'Echo' sculpture on your right, which is an exact reproduction of the hillside behind it - not a cast mirror image, but a reproduction. Now continue downhill to an intersection with a C2 marker on the left and a blue marker on the right. Cross straight over and, just after passing a forestry track to the right, you will come across 'Hill 33', which is rapidly returning to the Forest. Just past 'Hill 33' take the path off to the right (opposite a blue marker), going downhill to join a forestry track (B). Turn right, and immediately cross a wide outfall, looking to your right across the water to find the 'Cone and Vessel' sculpture, a large pine cone and acorn.

Keep on this track, passing a blue marker on the left, cross a stream and then come to a blue marker on your right, with a path opposite, going left into the trees. Take the path to a bench, and, sitting on the bench look up to your left to the sign on the tree, saying 'Silenzio'. Enjoy the quiet and then return to the track, turning left to keep going in the same direction you were headed before you made the detour. You soon come to another blue marker, on your right, and to the left you will see patches of bamboo. Stand at the entrance to the path on your left and look to your right, by the tree with the very knobbly trunk, to a circle of earth and a stone marker with an inscription saying 'Clear Circle, Define Border'. Now go down this path, cross the little stream (which may be dry in the summer), go between the bamboo clumps and follow the path as it goes up and to the left, until you come to a gate (C). Go through

Speech House

the gate, and you are now on the cycle trail (once a railway line). Turn left, and go along the trail, watching out for cyclists. Pass a blue marker and from here, keep an eye out on the left, down amongst the trees, for the life-sized 'Deer' sculpture. She is hard to spot, especially in summer when the trees are in leaf, but watch out for a line of old posts just below the cycle trail fence and when they end, look further into the trees and she is just in there.

Now keep on to the wooden barriers, going through to come to the 'Iron Road' with its beautiful Forest symbols - both natural and man-made - carved into the old sleepers. Go through the next barrier to reach White Gates (D). You will return to the gates, but first of all take a detour down the right hand path (not the main track, but the path indicated by the blue marker), going downhill a short distance to see 'Black Dome', a mound of black charcoal? earth? with short pieces of protruding logs. Follow the next blue marker, taking the path as it curves to the right towards a bench. Down on the left, by the man-made canal, is the sculpture 'Fire and Water Boats', a group of canoes sitting there in the shallow waters. Now follow the next blue marker to take the path uphill, going past one of nature's own sculptures - the trunk of a wonderful ancient beech tree whose top half, sheared off in some storm, lies in the dip behind. The path brings you out to the cycle trail, where you turn right to come back to the white gates (D).

Go through the gates and take the right hand track, then right again at the next fork. Go up the hill, pass one blue marker, and at the second marker follow the path to the left into the trees. Here you will find 'Dead Wood', a series of grave like stone slabs set in the forest floor. Return to the main track and continue up the hill to reach an intersection of tracks and a large signpost indicating various trails (E).

To stay on the walk, turn left, up the hill. Or you can make a short detour, taking the right hand track, then the first path left (following the blue arrows), to see the 'Heart of Stone' sculpture. If you do that, return to the signpost and then go up the short steep hill towards the site where 'Place' - the sculpture of what looked like a giant chair - used to be. The wide views over the valley and forest make this spot worthwhile in its own right, and they have kindly provided a bench so you can do this in comfort. With your back

Speech House

to the bench take the path towards a blue marker ahead of you. Follow this winding path, beautiful in autumn with its oak and beech, as it skirts above and around Beechenhurst, all the way to a gate.

If your dog has a tendency to run off and explore, put him on the lead now as for the rest of the walk you will parallel a very busy road, although you will hardly be aware of this. Go through the gate and keep on the path, shortly seeing the Speech House appearing through the trees up above you to the right. At a point where there is a sign pointing up a path to the hotel (F), go through the gate on your left, and a little way in you will come to a stand of yew trees, with a marker explaining their historical significance. Go back to the gate and turn left, continuing on until you reach the carpark.

A Walk from Soudley Ponds

Soudley Ponds is a series of man-made ponds set in a small steep-sided valley and surrounded by huge Douglas fir trees. The path around the ponds provides a beautiful and easy stroll for local people, visitors and dog walkers. There are no facilities, but the Dean Heritage Museum which is located on the opposite side of the road at the far end of the Ponds, has a cafe and dogs are welcome on the terrace.

Location: The carpark is located on the minor Soudley to Littledean Road, about a kilometre along on the right hand side (there is a sign as you turn into the parking area). OS Grid ref: SO668114

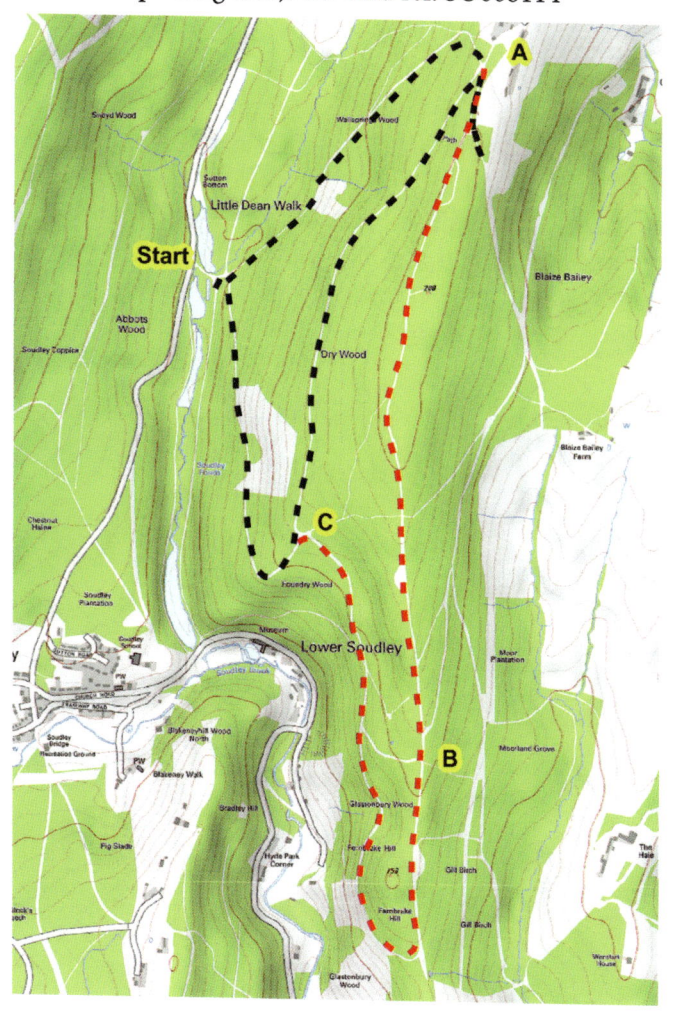

Soudley Ponds

> **Walks 12 and 12a Start point: carpark on the Soudley-Littledean Rd**
> 12: Length 3.8 km, total uphill walking 114 metres, est time 1 hr
> 12a: Length 5.8 km, total uphill walking 191 metres, est time 1½ hrs

This walk starts out with a fairly stiff climb, rewarded by the views across the Severn from the Blaize Bailey viewpoint. After that, it's all downhill, along a path which follows the contour of the hill – with some great forest views along the way–and then meets up with the longer option to descend to the carpark. The option undulates but gradually takes you back down via a large loop. There are lovely views across the valley in the latter part of the walk.

Walk through the barrier at the back of the carpark to a meeting of three forestry tracks. Take the middle track and climb steadily up to the top. As the track bends to the right, with a house on the left, you will see a path going off to the right. Pass this and continue up for a little way until you see a fork in the tracks and a yellow waymark pointing left (A). Follow the waymark and you immediately come to the Blaize Bailey viewpoint, giving you panaromic views across the Severn and up to the Cotswolds. Retrace your steps back to the fork.

The view from Blaize Bailey, Soudley Ponds

Soudley Ponds

Decision point

To continue the main walk, go back down to the path opposite the house. Turn left to follow the path gently downhill. You eventually come out at a forestry track (C). Opposite you is a grove of beech trees which are splendid in the autumn. Turn right on this track with the beech trees on your left, and wind your way downhill until you are back at the carpark.

Note: as of Nov 2015 both ends of this track had been churned up by logging operations. If it still looks wet, follow the option, looking out for a large cleared area on the right (great views), shortly after which you will see a waymarked path on the right. Take this straight down to reach point C. It's about the same time and distance as the main walk.

Option 12a

For the option, take the right hand track (as you face the post with the lookout on your left)) at the fork. From this point you simply continue on the main track, passing a number of paths on both sides. At one point another track comes in from the left (B) and after a while the track then sweeps downhill around to the right,

Soudley Ponds

giving you lovely views over the valley with some houses down below. There is a brief uphill shortly after this, going up to a grove of beech trees on the left. Here the track joins the path (on your right) from the main walk (C). Continue on the main track which bends around to the right and then winds its way downhill back to the carpark.

A Walk from Yorkley

There are numerous laybys beside most Forest roads where locals park to start their dog walks. I have chosen this one just outside the village of Yorkley as a good example of a "local walk".

> **Walks 13 and 13a Start point: Layby outside Yorkley, on the right just past the delimited speed signs heading towards Parkend.**
> *13: Length 3.7 km, total uphill walking 87 metres, est time 1 hr*
> *13a: Length 5.7 km, total uphill walking 147 metres, est time 1½ hrs*

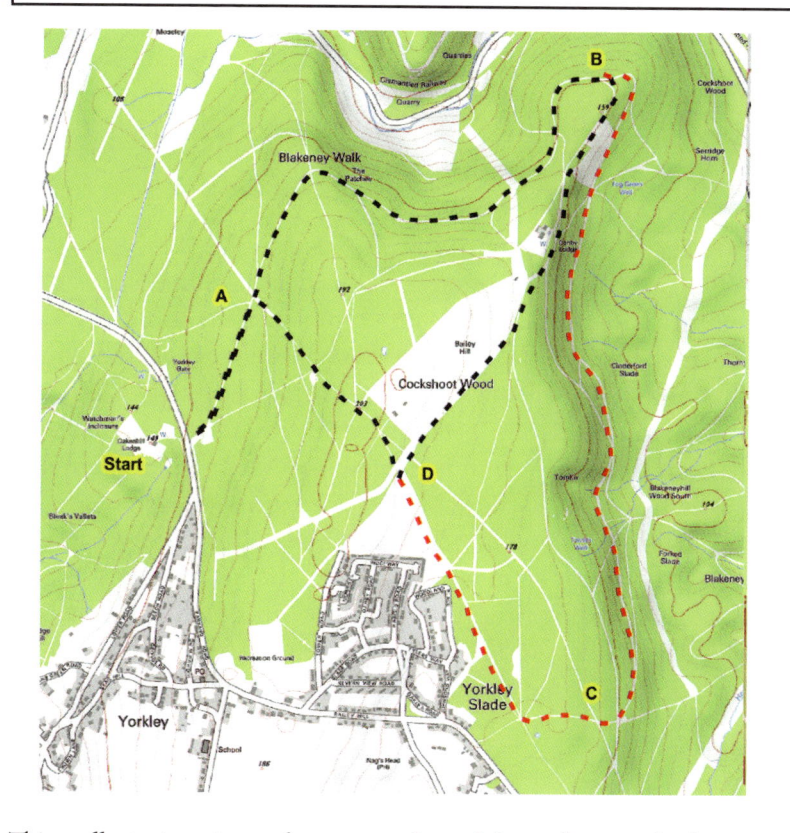

This walk starts out on a forestry track, and then takes you further up into the woods to go past Danby Lodge, formerly a forest manager's lodge and now a private home. Enjoy lovely views across the valley before descending via a grassy track back to your start point. The longer option misses Danby Lodge, but I have noted where you can make a short detour to see it if you wish.

Yorkley

Go through the barrier and along the track, with beech and oak to your right and conifers to the left. Pass under the telegraph wires and continue straight ahead, across an intersection with a path (A). Cross over the next path and continue on, passing a stile on your left as you follow the track around to the right. At this point the valley falls away quite steeply to your left. Go past an uphill path on your right and descend steadily. Pass another uphill track to the right and shortly afterwards pass under more telegraph wires. Follow the track until it climbs uphill and sweeps around to the right. As you reach the crest you will see that the track descends and curves right.

Decision point

To stay on the main walk, look out here for a wide path which goes up on your right (B).

Follow the path up and around to the right. A little way along there is a bench set at a point to take advantage of a spectacular view through the trees. The path climbs steadily to a fork. Keep left, passing Danby Lodge above you on your right and admiring the views to your left. At the next fork, keep right and pass through a gate next to a barrier. Here you can get a good view of the Lodge. Opposite you is a horse paddock. Take the forestry track which goes off to the left (NOT the path to the left of the forestry track) and follow that, keeping the paddocks on your right. Pass a track on your right which leads to some houses and shortly afterwards you come to an intersection with a path (D). The lines of telegraph poles also intersect here. Turn right and follow the instructions below for the main walk from point D.

Option 13a

For the option, continue downhill on the main track, continuing to bear right. The track winds its way around the contour of the hill with a number of rutted and steep logging tracks off to the right and left. Ignore all these and keep to the main track, which starts to ascend, at first gently and then more steeply. As the track levels out you come to a five way junction (C). Ignore the track immediately to your right, which heads back in the direction you have come from, and take the right hand track which goes up the hill. It's quite steep but soon levels out.

Cross an intersection with a path with a no riding symbol, continue on, ignoring another path to the right and noting the old quarry to your left. Go past a path to the left to reach a line of telegraph poles and a path off to the right with another no riding symbol. Take this path, following the line of telegraph poles through a grassy area with the outskirts of the village of Yorkley to your left. Keep following the telegraph poles to an intersection with a dirt road, with a couple of houses on the other side of the road and off to the right (D).

Cross the road and then follow the main walk instructions below. *Note: if you wish to see Danby Lodge, turn right along the dirt road and the Lodge is a short distance along, past the horse paddocks.*

Main walk continued

Go downhill on the path below the telegraph poles. Cross an intersection of paths, and continue on to the track at point A. Turn left and retrace your steps back to the layby.

Beechenhurst

A Walk from Beechenhurst

In the summer months Beechenhurst Lodge and picnic site attracts thousands of visitors every weekend and throughout the holidays. There is a cafe and toilets, barbecue facilities, a climbing wall and children's playground. There is also a Junior Go Ape ropes course. However, you don't need to go very far from the main site to get away from the crowds.

The Lodge used to be the site of Speech House Hill Colliery, a not very successful mine which was eventually acquired by the Crawshay family and used for ventilation and emergency exit purposes from other mines they owned nearby. The site was closed about 1945 and eventually transformed into the current Lodge and picnic area. In recent years the smooth grassy picnic grounds proved most attractive to boar, to such an extent that a (low key) boar proof fence has now been built around the whole area.

In addition to the walk described here you can follow the 4.5 miles long Sculpture Trail, which starts at Beechenhurst. (Visit www.forestofdean-sculpture.org.uk/sculptures for full descriptions of the various sculptures mentioned.)

You can also just do Option 14a, making the Speculation car park and picnic area your start point. And there is a 12.6 km walk from Beechenhurst included in the long walks section of this book.

Location: Beechenhurst is located between the Speech House and Coleford on the B4226. From the Speech House, head towards Coleford, going down the steep winding road. The turnoff to Beechenhurst is on your right and well marked. Parking is pay and display. The barrier is open and closed daily, with closing times varying depending on the time of year, so take note of the specific time as you drive in. OS Grid ref: SO614120

Speculation is located just off the B4234. Continue past Beechenhurst towards Coleford, turning right at the next intersection. Go past the Cycle Centre and Speculation is clearly marked not far beyond it on your right.

Beechenhurst

Walks 14, 14a Start point: Beechenhurst Lodge.
14: Length 3.8 km, total uphill walking 83 metres, est time 55 min
14a: Length 7.2 km, total uphill walking 138 metres, est time 1hr 40 min

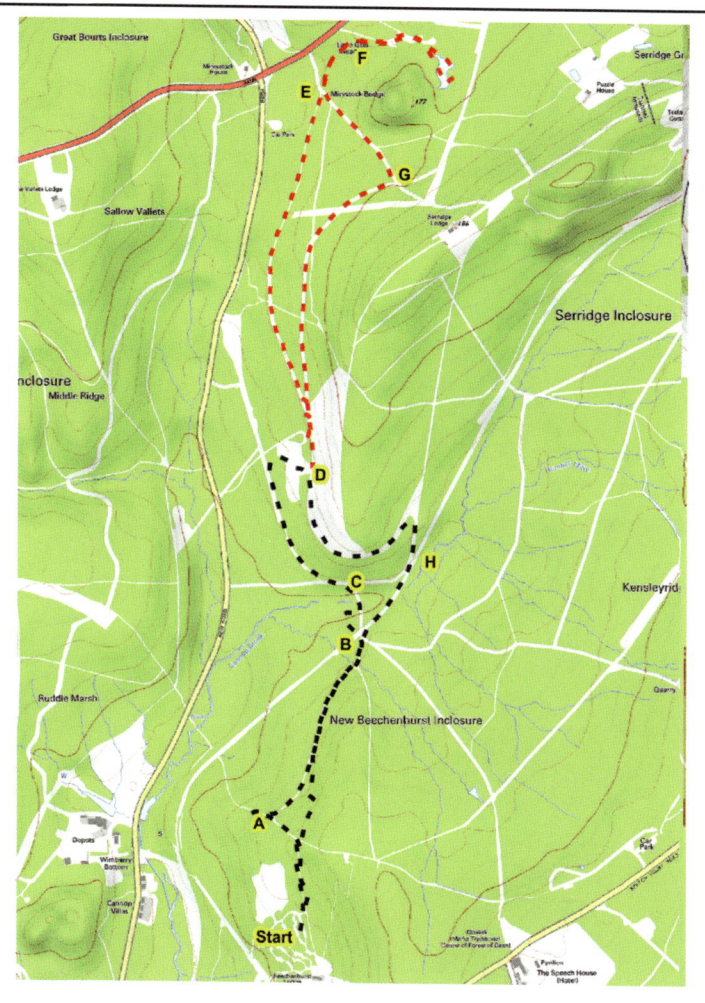

This relatively gentle walk combines good tracks with forest paths. It takes you to Speculation, the site of a coal mine which opened in 1800 and remained in production until 1925. The longer option takes in more industrial history, going past the Mierystock bridge and tunnel before leading you deeper into the Forest to walk around a delightful and peaceful fishing pond, which were once the Waterloo Colliery screens.

Beechenhurst

Facing the large Beechenhurst information map, take the path to the left, past the coach park and go through the boar-proof gate. Pass the Junior GoApe course and continue up the slope to a sign-posted intersection.

Turn left, going downhill to a red and blue marker (A). To see 'The Heart of Stone' sculpture follow the blue marker down the path a little way and off to the left, then come back up to the main track at point A. Turn left to continue down this track. Pass two blue markers. At the third blue marker the track curves gently to the right and goes more steeply downhill to a junction. On your right is a sign saying 'Shortcut A to Beechenhurst'. Ignore this (unless you want a very short walk), and follow the blue marker on your left down to the White Gates (B).

Go through the gate. Just to your left you will see another blue marker. Follow this to see the 'Black Dome' sculpture and, a little further along, the 'Fire and Water Boats' which are below the path at the side of the old industrial waterway. Keep following the blue markers back to the main track. The White Gates are off to your

Mierystock Tunnel

right, but turn left to the T-junction (C) with a cycle trail marker ahead of you.

Turn left and after about 60 metres turn right onto a narrow forest path. Follow this (the path can be damp underfoot in wet weather) to a fork. The path straight ahead goes to a dirt road, but keep right and come out on to a wide undulating grassy area. You will see the dirt road and parking area off to the left. You are now on the site of the former Speculation Colliery.

Follow the edge of the undergrowth around to the right to a small hill with a fenced off area on the top. Go up there to see the mine shaft. It's rather overgrown and surrounded by bracken so difficult to spot in the summer. Now return to the dirt road, turn right and start to take the right hand fork. Almost immediately there is a path on your right going uphill. Take this and turn right onto a wide track. You are now on the cycle trail (D).

Decision point

To stay on the main walk, turn right and follow this wide trail as it winds along the hill above a valley. It eventually makes a big right hand sweep, going downhill, and comes out at a signposted intersection with another part of the cycle trail (H). Cross over the intersection to turn right through the wooden barrier. Follow this past, or over, the beautiful 'Iron Road' sculpture. Go through another wooden barrier to come out at the White Gates (B).

Go back through the white gates and take the right hand track up to the fork with the sign saying 'Shortcut A to Beechenhurst'. *(You can take this shortcut, but be warned, it's quite a hill.)*

Take the right hand track, going back the way you came originally. Pass a blue marker on your right. Now follow the next blue marker left, to visit the 'Dead Wood' sculpture amongst the larch trees. Then return to the main track, turning left up the hill to come out at the signposted intersection. You can walk left up the track to the site where 'Place' (the Giant Chair) used to be, and admire the views across the Forest, and then follow the signs down

Beechenhurst

through the trees to return to Beechenhurst. Or simply walk down the track in front of you to pass through the boar gate to the Lodge and car park.

Option 14 a

For the longer option, turn left on the cycle trail at point D. After a short distance you come to a cycle trail signpost at a fork. Take the left fork, signposted Branch to Lydbrook. Now follow this trail for some way, looking out on your right for a fenced in mine entrance and also a pile of red bricks – traces of the area's industrial past. Eventually you come to Mierystock Bridge (E). Just before the bridge there is a gap in the fence and a narrow path leading down into the cutting and under the bridge. Go for an explore if you wish, but then return to the trail. *(Note: If it's very dry you may be able to walk under the bridge to the tunnel ahead, but mostly it's quite wet down there. In any case, you still need to come back up again.)*

The detour to the fishing ponds starts here, so if you don't wish to follow this, pick up the instructions again at point E below.

Continue on the trail, past the Mierystock Tunnel and its viewing point, and shortly come to a point where the trail bends left, with a rough path going off to the right (it's very rough and can be very muddy as well) (F). Take this right hand path and follow it to an open area. Go straight across to a forest track and turn right, following the track to where it splits and loops back on itself (a turning area for vehicles). On your right is a path which will bring you to the edge of the fishing pond. Once upon a time these were colliery screens, where the coal was washed and graded after being brought to the surface. This is a beautiful and tranquil spot, despite the ever present hum of traffic behind you. You can walk around the edge to take in the different perspectives (be careful not to head off at a tangent into the woods), or you can just stop awhile and enjoy the rest.

Now retrace your steps: go back to the track, turn left and then left again to cross the open area and then take the path back to the

Beechenhurst

Waterloo Colliery Screens

cycle trail. Turn left and return to Mierystock Bridge (E).

Cross the bridge and continue straight on, through a wooden barrier, going gently uphill on a stony path. To your right is a spoil heap, now just part of the Forest. The path brings you out on to a wide track, which is part of the cycle trail (G). Turn right and go gently downhill. Pass Speculation on your right and rejoin the main walk at the decision point, D.

Longer Walks

A Long Walk from Beechenhurst

See Walks from Beechenhurst for general information and directions.

Walk 15 Start point: Beechenhurst Lodge
Length 12.6 km, total uphill walking 274 metres, est time 3¼ hrs

A good three hour or so ramble through the Forest, taking in old colliery sites in various stages of disappearance, along forest paths and wider tracks, with (mostly) gentle slopes and open views over heathland and through trees. A good day's outing and the dog will love it too. You have to cross a busy road, so remember the lead.

Longer Walks

Facing the large Beechenhurst information map, walk up the right hand main trail ahead. Go through the heavy wooden gate in the boar proof fence and continue up the winding path until you reach the top and a Beechenhurst Trail marker with a yellow arrow and a blue arrow pointing left (A). Turn left to the bench. This is where 'Place' - the much loved sculpture otherwise known as the Giant's Chair - used to be. There's a little memorial plaque there now but the wide views over the valley and forest make the short climb worthwhile in its own right.

Continue on past the bench to the main track, and turn left following the blue marker downhill to the signpost. Keep straight on in the direction Sculpture Trail 'Heart of Stone' and where the track does a sweep to the right, keep left, following the blue and red marker. The track now becomes a path, and a little way ahead the 'Heart of Stone' sculpture is off to your left (follow the blue arrow). Admire it, then return to the path, continuing downhill then steeply and briefly uphill to go through a gate and onto the cycle trail (B).

Note: if the weather has been very wet, the next section of the walk will be quite muddy. To avoid this, you can turn right on the cycle trail to reach White Gates, then turn left at the signpost in the direction Drybrook Road Station, then left again at the T-junction. About 60 metres along look out for a narrow path off to your right. This is point C. Take the path, following the directions from point C below.

Cross the cycle trail, go over the stile (the dog goes under the fence) and down the path with a wooden fence on the left. The path now becomes uneven and muddy in places, even in dry weather, but it takes you through a pretty valley with a stream running through it. At the end of the fence, bear slightly left and head downhill towards the road (there is a choice of paths) to a footbridge which you can see at the bottom of the valley. Don't cross the bridge, but turn right just before it and follow the path as it winds its way along to eventually reach another footbridge - note the old man-made drainage channels to the left. Cross this bridge and follow the path to the right, going steadily uphill and coming out at a wide forestry track. Turn right onto the track and

Longer Walks

go uphill to the crest, where there is a narrow path going at a sharp angle off to your left (C). If you come to the cycle trail signpost you have gone too far.

Take the narrow path, which in summer can be quite overgrown and in winter can be rather puddly. Near the end, bear right at the fork to come out to a wide grassy area. This is Speculation (see Walk 14 if you wish to try and see the old mine shaft). Cross over the grass to the road and carpark and at the fork in the road, take the left track. Pass a wide but generally muddy path on the left and then take the next narrow path left up to the cycle trail. Turn left, and at the signpost take the left hand fork in the direction Branch to Lydbrook. Now follow this path for some distance to Mierystock Bridge, paralleling the line of the old railway (D). *Note: if you wish to see Waterloo Screens, follow the instructions in Walk 14a.*

Turn right over the bridge, noting the tunnel in the cutting to your left. Go through a wooden barrier and walk steadily uphill to an intersection with the cycle trail, and where some clear felling has recently taken place. *Note: The path straight ahead, through the clear felled area, is slowly recovering and you may take it if you wish, to go*

Longer Walks

straight up, through the barrier to the forestry track with Serridge Lodge on your right. If it's still a quagmire, follow the instructions below.

Turn left to shortly reach a T-junction. Turn right, then follow the path to the left, going around the fallen tree if they still haven't removed it. The path climbs very steeply for a short way to a barrier. Go through onto a forestry track. Serridge Lodge, one of the old Forestry Lodges, is off to your right. Turn left, past another barrier, then continue on this track along the ridge line with lovely views to the left in winter. Pass a stile on your right and about 200 metres further on, turn right down a track which takes you past Trafalgar Lodge. Follow the track around to the left - noting the stones on your right which mark the site of the Trafalgar colliery - and go past the houses onto a narrow path. The chance of sighting deer along this path are quite high. Keep going for some way until you eventually come to a metalled track. Turn right and go a short distance to Drybrook Road Station, at an intersection with the cycle trail (E).

Turn left, in the direction Dilke Bridge, and keep on the cycle trail to an intersection marked by hazard posts. *Note: if you wish to take a shortcut, continue straight ahead and follow the cycle trail markers to Dilke Bridge, point G.*

Turn right, uphill, and continue on this track to a metal barrier. Go through and come out at a high spot where a metalled track intersects with a number of paths. The views across the open heathland are wonderful and you may well spot deer in there also (F).

Turn left and stay on the metalled track until the tarmac ends at a point where the track bends sharply to the right with a yellow waymark pointing right. Don't follow the waymark, but turn left onto another metalled surface which soon degenerates into a rough dirt track which slopes gently upwards to a junction with another path. Continue straight on, with open cleared land to your right , and an enclosure to your left.

Pass a gate into the enclosure and then, as the track bends to the right you will see, on your left, another gate into the enclosure. Between

Longer Walks

you and the gate is a path. Cross over to the path and turn right to follow it past the end of the enclosure. Keep on, going downhill to reach another open area with views of Cinderford off to the left. Go past the end of another enclosure and keep on for a little way until you come to a fork. Take the grassy path to the left, soon going downhill, and negotiate a small muddy patch to come out on to the cycle trail. Turn right and follow the trail to Dilke Bridge (G).

Just after the bridge, turn right at the signpost to follow the direction Cannop Wharf and Cycle Centre. Go past Lightmoor Colliery (you may spot a peacock and/or a pig), through the gate and straight on up the hill to a T-junction. Turn right to go through the large stones and follow the track, curving to the left at the point where it becomes more of a grassy path straight ahead, and coming out at a junction of paths. Take the right hand track to an intersection with a large oak in the middle and a marker saying M3 on the right. Continue straight on. At the next intersection, again keep straight on, and again at the next intersection, which will lead you to the Arboretum. Go through the gate and straight across to the exit (H). Or you may choose to have a look around, and perhaps take advantage of the benches to have a short break.

Once you leave the Arboretum (with your dog on its lead) follow the track up to the main road, taking the left hand fork. You will see the Speech House off to your left. Cross the road into the grassy area straight ahead. Be very careful - the traffic moves fast here. There is no path, but keep the small wooden enclosure (which appears to be protecting holly and brambles) on your right, and walk straight down until you can see a path below you and to the left. Head for the path - you have to scramble down a short but steep bank - and when you reach it, turn left and follow the blue and yellow markers. Pass a Speech House sign pointing back up to the road - and keep on, going downhill, to pass through a wooden gate. Pass a white marker, then a commemorative oak on your left. Immediately after the oak, ignore the blue marker which points right and take the narrow, and somewhat steep, downhill path on your left. Follow this to a gate in the boar proof fence, go through the gate, and you are back at Beechenhurst, on the opposite side of the Lodge from the main carpark.

Longer Walks

A Long Walk from Mallards Pike

See Walks from Mallards Pike for general information and directions.

> **Walk 16 Start point: Mallards Pike car park**
> *Length 13.5 km, total uphill walking 235 metres, est time 3 ¼ hrs*

This long walk takes in many aspects of the Forest, walking on wide tracks, narrow paths which wend through quiet woods, and parts of the cycle trail. It involves quite a lot of steady uphill work in the first half, rewarded with wide views, but also offers the opportunity to visit a beautiful lake (mud permitting). Make sure you take the dog's lead as you have to cross a busy road twice.

Longer Walks

With the Go Ape office on your left, walk to the beginning of the Running Trail and continue on until the track divides into three. Take the right hand path and continue along this undulating and slightly winding track for some time until you come to a T-junction. Towards the end, the forest has been cleared to your right and you may see deer or foxes in here. Turn right and, passing a track off to your right, go up the hill to a metal gate and stile (the stile can be avoided by scrambling up the bank to the left of the gate) (A). Cross the stile to a junction of tracks, and turn left. Now follow this track for some distance, winding up and downhill, passing a couple of enclosures with young beech. In the summer there are foxgloves and, later, large rosebay willow herb, in amongst the beech and the occasional rowan with their rich red berries. The track slopes down and comes to a fork, where you keep left, continuing downhill. Cross a stream with a path running alongside and continue uphill. As you crest the hill you will see Cinderford ahead of you. Go down to the road, putting your dog on the lead on the way (B).

Across the road to your right is the entrance to Linear Park. But you are going to go straight across the road to a narrow path in the grass, just to the left of the telegraph pole, and hard to see from this side. Be very careful - the road is busy, traffic moves fast and there is a blind bend to the right.

Go along the narrow path towards a metal gate into a rugby field. Just before the gate, turn left to wend your way uphill through the trees, coming out onto a path which is the cycle trail. Turn right and head along the trail to where there are two cycle trail markers in quick succession - the first indicates a downhill path to the right, but keep on to the second marker where there is also a sign saying Family Cycle Trail and a white arrow pointing up the path. Turn left to follow the white arrow to reach another intersection with the cycle trail and a signpost. Turn right in the direction Drybrook Road Station and follow the trail, passing the remains of Foxes Bridge Colliery, to an intersection with hazard posts (C).

Turn left here, uphill. The track levels out after a while and then

Longer Walks

takes you to a metal barrier. Go through the barrier and onto a metalled track, admiring the views across the Forest which suddenly open up in front of you.

Cross the metalled track to the stone marker and then take the diagonal path which is immediately to the right of the marker (not the path with yellow waymarks), crossing the heathland to arrive at a wide forestry track (D). This is another good place to spot deer, and sometimes foxes.

At this point you have a choice. If the weather has been reasonably dry and you don't mind a bit of rough, possibly muddy, walking, then follow the instructions in the next paragraph. The reward for your effort is to walk around the beautiful and mostly hidden Woorgreen Lake. Woorgreen is the result of open cast mining which took place in this very swampy area up until 1981. Rather than refill the hole, they let it fill with water and it's now a beautiful nature reserve. However, much of the path is terrible in winter and in very wet weather, slippery with clay and rutted, and is not to be recommended. So, if that's the case, turn right at point D and follow the track as it bends to the left, goes past a small pond and

Longer Walks

then to an intersection. Turn left, go through the gate ahead and continue up, walking alongside the high hedge which surrounds Kensley Lodge until you reach the gate into the Lodge, with paths off to your right. This is point E. Follow the instructions from point E below.

To walk around Woorgreen, from point D turn left and head towards the trees about 100 metres up on your right. Just past the point where the trees start, take the wide but rough path to the right (this is the worst section so if it's passable, the rest should be). Follow this alongside a little stream and ahead you will soon catch a glimpse of the lake. At a T-junction with yellow waymarks, turn right and take the grassy path which parallels the lake. Follow the path around to another yellow waymark pointing right. There is a notice here asking you not to allow your dog into the water at this point. Turn right and then right again at the intersection to take the path out. (If you would like to give the dog a swim, carry on around the lake edge for about 50 metres to an area set aside for a dog dip.) Turn right at the intersection and follow this rough path back, past a yellow waymark, to a gate near the high hedge surrounding Kensley Lodge. Turn left and walk alongside the hedge until you reach the gate into the Lodge, with paths off to your right (E).

From point E, follow the blue markers to the 'Cathedral' sculpture, then turn right along this path to a carpark. Go through the carpark and down to the road, dog on the lead.

Go about 10 metres to your right along the verge and then cross very carefully to a barely discernible path which wends through these trees to the Arboretum carpark which you can see ahead of you. Go into the Arboretum and turn right, following the path to the gate at the far end. Go through the gate, turn left and go through another gate onto a wide forestry track. This is Spruce Ride (F).

From point F, follow the Ride straight down, crossing over the first intersection and then walking between the huge cherry trees

Longer Walks

(gorgeous in spring, full of luscious fruit for the taking in summer) to the second intersection, with Speech House Lake on your right. Turn right towards the lake but then turn immediately left, and follow this path with the lake and the fishing stands on your right and the stream on your left.

Just where the path begins to curve to the right, following the lake, the path forks. Take the left fork to stay alongside the little stream. It winds its way through the trees, crosses the stream and then goes along beside a fence to reach a forestry track. Turn right, go over the stream again and then continue up the hill ahead of you to a junction at the crest with a sign saying Trafalgar Avenue on your right (G).

Stay left and a little over 100 metres along, take the path which goes left through the pine trees and come out at a narrow, grassy track. Turn left, downhill to reach a track parallel with the cycle trail. Turn right and you will soon come to T-junction, where you do a dog leg left then right, to go onto the cycle trail at a point where there is a signpost. Follow the signpost in the direction Mallards Pike 1.5 km. The trail narrows and bends to the left and then comes out at a wide track. Turn right and follow the various trail signs straight on to Mallards Pike.

Ten Short walks

The following walks don't need maps. They are short, easily accessed and on good tracks, and are listed here for those who have puppies which can't go for long walks yet, or for dog walkers with limited mobility, or if you have a stroller/toddler as well as a dog to handle. They're also great for when the dog's already had one proper walk that day and you just need to take him around the block, as it were.

Bathurst Park, Lydney
Whitecross Road, Lydney GL15 5DQ

A cafe and children's play area (no dogs) with a large open park beyond where dogs can run off lead.

Cannop Ponds
See Walk 7 for directions and detailed information

Stroll along the cycle trail as far as the stone works, and back again

Linear Park, Cinderford
See Walk 6 for directions and detailed information

Stroll along the main track for as far as you wish, and back again.

Lydney Lake
Lakeside Gardens, Lydney GL15 5RH. Hidden between the rugby club and the bypass, parking on Lakeside Gardens or nearby.

Stroll around, making sure your dog doesn't disturb the fishermen.

Lydney Harbour
Harbour Road, Lydney GL15 4ER (continue on past the Station as far as you can go)

Walk around this Ancient Scheduled Monument and/or take the canal path towards Lydney and back again.

Mallards Pike
See Walk 4 for directions and detailed information.

Walk around the Lake or follow the Running Trail for a distance, and then walk back again.

Short Walks

Soudley Ponds
See Walk 12 for directions and detailed information

Walk around the ponds, crossing over either at the first bridge, or, for something longer, the second bridge. Take care not to let your dog disturb the fishermen.

Speech House Arboretum
See Walk 9 for directions and detailed information

Very popular dog walking in a large (and enclosed) space.

Spruce Ride
Signposted entrance to carpark on the road from the Speech House heading towards New Fancy and Parkend. Or walk through the Arboretum, and Spruce Ride is to the left as you go through the far gate.

This wide Ride is worth a visit in the spring when the cherry trees are in full bloom. Walk down and back up again.

Wenchford
See Walk 1 for directions and detailed information.

Walk down to and through the picnic area, up the ramp and back to the carpark; or take the track from the carpark straight along to Blackpool Bridge and then return, via the picnic area if you wish.

Printed in Great Britain
by Amazon